WHO'S WATCHING WHOO? READINGS TO SLOW ME DOWN

COME AWAY MOMENTS FOR MYSELF

JOHN BRAGSTAD

COMPASS SEASON

40 SHORT CHAPTERS / NATURE'S INSPIRATION

"For John Bragstad, the woods, water, plants, animals—the whole of nature—is his compass, and he captures it beautifully in his thoroughly terrific book *Compass Season.*

A quintessential poet, John's prose comes through on each and every page. The book is 214 pages long, well sourced, and is easy to read in one sitting or, you can read chapters in season or out of the season they were written for and be blessed." *Cook County News-Herald.*

"*Compass Season* by North Shore resident John Bragstad, a collection of 40 seasonal short stories and 'a gem of a book.'" *Minneapolis Star-Tribune.*

> "*Eloquently written by Grand Marais resident John Bragstad, we are reminded to slow down and appreciate the world around us.*"
> *Northern Wilds magazine*

A great book to throw in a backpack, take with you on vacation, enjoy next to a cozy fire, or have on your nightstand to slow down before sleep.

Available at Amazon.com or in local Grand Marais bookstores.

To those who come away
disappointed with pictures
they have taken of grand and
magnificent wilderness ...

but who do it anyway.

Publisher's Cataloging the publication
John Bragstad

Previously Published as *Nature's Poetry of Life: Who's Watching Who? Northern Free Verse Poetry.*

Reprinted as *Who's Watching Whoo? Readings to Slow Me Down / Come Away Moments For Myself*

ISBN 13: ISBN: 978-0-9996854-3-3

CONTACT THE AUTHOR AT P.O. Box 248, Grand Marais, MN 55604. Or go to **johnbragstad.com**

Please Note:

The content of this book is for information purposes and should **not** be construed as advice. If you are seeking help, consult with a professional therapist who can tailor treatment to your individual needs.

Any resemblance to a specific person is purely coincidental except in chapters where that person has been named explicitly.

I am a great admirer
of mystery and magic.

Look at this life -
all mystery and magic.

Harry Houdini

PROLOGUE: SONGS TO OUR SELVES

We all have interior melodies,
waiting canvasses eager to fill.
Uncertain paths where we must
strike out
to discover
where they lead,
where they betray us,

where they dissolve
into unanimity.

We learn to trust
these quiet instigations.
We step away
to listen.

We stand aside
to marvel
at tilted flowers,

blossoms born
from uncertain seed.

We watch endings
fade and deliver,
undetermined
until
they reveal
themselves.

We wait for words
to fulfill the longings
we feel,

trapped within,
bundled by
snares of
word invention
and insistent spirit.

Gently
to lay these aside,
to believe
we will not be
orphaned.

A blade of leaf,
A bed of grass, there
in the undergrowth,
a fawn watches
eyes wide open,

spotted only

by those who
wait and who know

things such as this
might be seen.

WHO'S WATCHING WHOO?

He found me.
This single chickadee
perched outside
my second story
window.

Reminder the bird feeder
had gone dry. Insistence
on the wing.

Winter cold for breakfast.
Tiny hearts beating fast.
Waiting entirely too long
for the symphony of
sunflower seeds
to begin.

Nature's venture
into my bedroom
of warm covers and

nestled comfort.

Who is watching Whoo?
Who gains from this mismatch?

I, the Master of the Feast?
Or these inhabitants
of the silent spaces,
welcoming me
to the serene
and simple,

touchpoints
I require
in a world spinning
and assaulting me
with its clamor?

CONTENTS

I

SUMMER'S GLORY

SUMMER'S GLORY

Bright gracing water,
Smiling to the sun's first kiss,
We welcome you.

To a land that is weary
we have waited,
and watched,
longing for release.

It is an alien sun we feel,
its warmth we cherish,
its light gives breathing room
to our day.

Oh summer, we wrest from you
all the energy of our brave new spirits.

You have found us.
We welcome you.
We welcome your invitation

to live again in exult and hyperbole.

We translate our fears into joy.
We wrest what was broken
from idling despair.

The sultry sun embraces us.
For moments we are whole.
We lift our faces to the sky
and wonder at the gifts we
have been given.

Oh summer, shine on us.
Remind us there is promise
in the budding of a leaf,
in the advent of each new day.

FIRST LIGHT

In the pale first reflection,
daylight approaches.

it comes to us quietly,
slow and soft.

It wakes us from shadow,
it prods us with rude intent,
bathed in the fresh opening of a new day.

First light invites adventure.
It rouses us to make ready.
It gifts us with sleepy cups of coffee,
it reminds us it will not be there for long.

We take to the trail.
We watch the day dwindle down.

Long hours meant for laughter,
abandoned comfort for swimming,

fish that fry clean,
freedom,
relief,
songs to my inner self
shared in the songs of others.

Water-weary,
remnants of misery,
carry-over portage madness,
taking us to distant places,
towards hospitality and home.

We rise, eager to taste
the fruit the first light offers us.

We wish for promise.
We see in the unfolding
of the new day

restless inhibition,
wandering license,

furtive imagination
launched within the sands of time.

WAKE-UP MORNINGS

The strong tincture of the
sun rolling out of bed,
the bird song
breaking to the east,
coffee growling on the stove,
I, eager to answer.

The world saturated in green,
cars moving to the sound of adventure,
the taste of dereliction in the air,
the breath of uncommon good.

Lake smells,
Campfire smells,
the invitational pull of the garden
offering its rich scent of soil
and promise.

Summer dwells on the horizon of

each new and uncertain day.
It lingers as it waits for us
to embrace its beauty.

It shares its magic
with the distressed,
the arrogant,
the rich and poor,
the embittered
and hollow,
the distracted,

with those who watch
and who choose
wonder.

Days glide by
but mornings
introduce
themselves,
shake our hand,
and ask us to recall their
name at day's close-out.

The crow's sharp cawing,
the eager moon waiting
to extend its light to
far-flung places,
the staccato notes of
the rain on the roof,

fresh sunlight,

are but small talk
seeking a deeper friendship.

Mystery's invitation
to the Dance.

MERRY GOLD

Marigolds first appear in the ditches
Far before the summer crowd.

They are the first to signal
the birth of spring.

They lie in low places,
move from the muck and
drainage to the sunlight
and to raised recognition.

They reflect the sun.

They are the celebration
of life at the bottom of a
nondescript ditch.

They compete with the browns
and plainer language of a pine forest
in early April and May.

They are harbingers of what is to come.
Heralds of another, brighter day.
They compete with no one.
They are the original, the first.
They proclaim the colors
in a world of grey,
a world of frost and fading ice.

They wait for no cue,
they advance with elaborate design.
They occupy the low places.
They are longed for as
first announcers of spring.

They do not apologize
for their lowly status.
Nature has selected them,
and they are equal
to their diminutive task.

Broadcasters of new life
in a weary and forlorn world.

SOFT MOON / JUNE'S PERSUASION

Brave originator
of the night,
casting its light
into an ever
deepening
day.

It sails across
the glooming,
fleeting colors
of starlight.

It watches and waits.

We must be willing to say,
we cannot tend her,
this frail moon.

Soft,

Still,
at the end of
a summer's day

It lingers,
and casts its
shadow.

It haunts romance
and crouches to
overtake the
unsuspecting.

For a moment we are
entranced, caught in a
magicians web of
wonder and interested
intrigue.

Pale it glows
but full,
an envoy reaching
to engage us in mutual conversation,
love's lost and found.

About life's leisure
and walking tall amidst
the pines of our regret.

Moon flailing to hold
its bright position in the sky,
how lovely, how poignant,
how ancient eyes have

searched and discovered
remnants of an ancient home,
caressed and compelling.

6

RISING

Shallow habitants of the stream bed,
ingenious planners of when to strike.
They laze in rapid waters,
patient anticipation,
willing aptitude.

Splendent colors
intermingled with the sun,
shadowed in dark pools
tempted and tempting.

Flashed to the surface,
waters breaking.
Lashed to the torrent.
Insects must resign themselves.

They rise,
opportunists all,
breath of speckled silver,
iridescent neon on a

field of mottled green.

Mystical hunters of the forest glen,
Wandering minstrels
of the poetic mind.

Creel caught,
Memory-laced
with passion.
Born of solitude.

7

MORNING BIRDSONG

Rousing wake-up chorus,
Notes interspersed throughout the dawn.
Bright melodies,
Seeking answers.
Searching questions,
in shadows
softer light
advancing.

Weathering the night,
in quiet,
a world transformed.

Night breaks-fast with the
silence.
On the move again but wait.
One more note,
one individual song,
one song among others.

Boldly shouted
Unself-consciously proclaimed.

Well-mannered.
Unworried.
Comfortable.
Generous in its gift to me.

Nature's musical score
to pale yellows
and lavenders,
a wash of blues and grays

Painting the lake's surface
in daylight.

8

WILD FLOWERS

It is the thick of the summer.
The wild flowers
are celebrating.

From out of the grandfather rock
with its stoic brown faces,
from the black, bleak surfaces
of the precambrian,
they come.

Yellows and rusts and golds,
blues that set the
sky on notice,
brave pinks and purples,
they are all here
born of winter.

They are unapologetic
of their small stature,
their diminutive

frame.

They are in a rare mood
Bright with possibility,
aflame with color,
the urgency of life
chasing itself
in the morning's
rising.

It is a grand get-together.
A soiree of guests
wandering the grounds,
mingling, mixing,
thrown together by
slow winds and
sultry restlessness.

They capture today.
They are foundlings
of a torrid sun,
parched,
passionate,
persistent,
pleasing.

Oh world!
How rich that we
can squander our sight
on the road ahead

while the shindig
carries on
beneath our feet.

9

DANDELION SUMMER

They are a poor man's flower,
bereft of innocence,
common,
everywhere.

They propagate,
blazing yellows
in fields of green,
tarnished by
their unwanted
presence.

The world can ill afford
the time to be
rid of them.

They are an
inconvenience
of summer.

They grow stubborn
to the wayward will
of tenders who
know better,
who have decided
extinction
would be best.

They live on false promises.
They grow in fervent hope.
They share the sun,
covet the rain as much
as any other.

Flowers there are,
consigned to table and porch,
coteries of culture,
gatherings of the refined,
celebrity watched,
admired,
discovered.

But there,
in the glooming light,
outlaws on the run
sow their profligate seed,
fix their roots deep

and declare
they will not be brushed
so easily aside.

The life force is theirs also.
Irresistible,

Demanding,
Insistent and
Proud.

It will not retreat
from a world
so little understood,
so careful in its
approbation
and deceit.

BASEBALL IN A NORTHERN TOWN

Base runners,
like rifle-shot,
ready to go
if the catcher
can't corral
a wild-bronco
pitch.

Arching fly balls
caught on the run
in left center,
surprised
ecstacy.

Deliberate pitchers,
care-worn
with responsibility,
bright young faces
overshadowed by
the metric of

balls and
strikes.

Eager parents
waiting on their
child's success,
eye's aflame
in their own
memory.

Baseball.
On a field of dreams,
Small-town America's
signature.

Sandlot once removed,
athletes still in runners.
Soft summer nights,
drifting through daylight.

Laughter still at the careless throw
back to the pitcher's mound.

Quiet acceptance
of the umpire's call,
Brave walk to the dugout
under the watchful glance
of a coach's smiling eyes.

A miss. "But at least
you swung at that pitch!"
Rewarded effort,
Life's lesson learned.

Rocketed throw from third,
into the embrace of a first-
baseman's glove.
Deep satisfaction,
mutually shared.
Life lesson #2.

A faint glimpse of disapproval
when a pitch fails outside
the umpire's strike zone.
But the game moves on.
Lesson #3.

Joy and sadness,
Disapproval and resolve,
Disappointment and glory.
The rules of the game.

Who covers second on a hit
up the middle with a man
on first?

All encompassed in this field
of mostly green and sand.

Fretful urgency
waiting for
and watching their
children grow up.

Scuffed baseballs
returned to the umpire's hand
because now they know better.

Still, a young person's game,
with the world waiting on-deck.

Innocence at play
Rounding third
And headed for home.

11

LOON LAUGHTER

Warbling up great canyons,
drifting over silent spaces of time.

When the moon fills,
when the night is soft,
loon laughter transforms
wildness into song.

It calls to another.
It dances on the
webbed feet
of the wind.

It mates whispering silence
to sound, reckless
and uninhibited,
primitive and
unbroken,
indigenous,
rowdy,

untouched.

Loon laughter echoes proudly over the hills.
It seeps into the cracks of untamed places.
It is reluctant to go to domesticated venues.
It watches purposefully over the North.

Wait for it.
Be ready for it.
Silence when it speaks.
Know you are listening
to the early,
distant sounds
of our first genesis.

We want it to last but then,
night swallows it up
in its ethereal embrace.

Testing the waters for truth,
measuring creation for its worth,
watchful of wilderness,
witness to God's humor.

In tremolo,
haunting sounds
and unrehearsed
yodels.

12

PRESENTIMENT

It is the apex of summer.
Trees celebrate.
The water is wide
and even.

Sailboats are in casual stride
up towards Isle Royale
or across to the Apostles.

It is a time of play,
of resurgence,
of deft companionship
and outrageous
melody.

But one day soon,
appearing,
couched in the grass
or in the bevy of
tree canopy,

a speckled leaf
will appear,
orange and
sometimes
yellow.

It will shout
the coming of
autumn,
the change in
character,
the disruption
of joy and
relaxed candor.

As suddenly,
life will become
more serious,
more deliberate,
more sober.

While not there yet,
the seasons will announce
a chilling amplitude.

Ducks foraging will be alerted
to soon migration.
Beavers might pick up the pace.
Canoeists might guard what
little time they have left
in the border country,
among the pines.

Life is altered.

With the coming of
that single leaf,
we know our
perspective
is changing.

We watch ever more deliberately
for life's advantages, we wait
ever more aware of tomorrow's
benedictions.

We grow mindful of the time,
keep watch over our anxiousness
and sorrow, while we yet celebrate
this festival of emerging color.

Summer shapes itself
into harvest-time.

We accept its eternal pace,
step in line to its rhythm,
reluctant acceptance,
yet fearful of the disquiet
one leaf can bring.

TODAY THE BERRIES

Today the berries must be picked,
Tomorrow will not do,
the sun has tinged them perfect blue,
the next days might be fleeting.

Today the berries must be picked,
in undiscovered places,
off paths seldom traveled
such unexpected graces.

Delayed wildness will not work.
Tomorrows chores can wait.
Today is for the sending,
tomorrow for the mending,

heavy on the branch,
wine-stained hands,
treasures not to shirk.

Today the berries must be picked,
Bursting flavor, luscious melody
for any pastry or delight,

A sometimes accidental
favor in plain sight.

II

DRIFTWOOD

1

DRIFTWOOD

Driftwood finds its way to an uneven cove,
Who knows what stories it can tell?

Of places where it owned its native land,
Of other harbors far from its resting place.

It traveled on the tide of wave and wind.
It bleached its bones in the winter sun.
It found refuge unevenly,
tentatively.
Waiting for a contrary breeze
to lift from these stones,
to journey.

Dry tinder it makes
in storm-crested weather.
It satisfies the hungry soul
combing the shore.

It waits for no one,

watches blankly,
joins reluctantly,
fires exuberantly.

It adorns the rocky strand,
slips in, in secret
rides with the waves
and complains but softly.

The surly sea, big or small,
is of no consequence.
Drifting it divides its anger,
pausing it waits
for the wind to rise.

For the waves to say,
"Let us be gone."

2

1876

Isle Royal
drawn from a
surveyor's hand.

Coffee-stained brown,
crouching beside
its bleached middle.
Untouched,
parchment-colored.

Royal instead of Royale.
From soundings recorded
on original sheets.
Siskiwit, Rock Harbor,
Washingon,

giving good protection
except for winds from Nor'West;
With good holding grounds
for wary ships and sailboats.

Fort William, Port Arthur,
original names with
Thunder Bay waters
to the East.
A reference point:
Grand Portage
almost hidden,
below.

And Parkerville
now extinguished.

Grateful map,
found it's way home,
from office and chart room.

its frame tells you it is lifted
from operational status
to wall.
glazed black-burnished frame.
tired,
examined,
broken canvas,
mouse-like scratchings,
nibbling at its edges.

Brought to my cabin-home,
from a thousand miles away.
Rescued,
returned
to native soil,
to places it remembers
vividly
in tenured sleep.

Declination lines
and dangers,
first efforts
to mark
a wild
and unknown
land.

3

VISION

Caught within the embers of a fire,
Long thoughts,
distant questions,
breaking visions,
wandering persuasions.

Left in the silence of the night,
we pause to search within
the fire's glow.

We wait for nature's light.
Ideas dance,
Memories arise,
Lazily drift
one to another.

We are warmed
by conversations with our selves.
Fragments tossed together
of broken dreams,

soft utterances,
wandering questions,
dream-catchers
blended into night air.

Smoke arises.
Quiet informs the land.
This little confessional,
This birthing place.

Home to tomorrows possibility.
Before I rest,
live coals draw me ever in,
the moment invites discovery.

4

MY DOG JACK

I whisper his name
and his one ear pivots
to take in the sound,
to respond.

Contrary at times,
watchful,
ready and playful
he waits
to walk me through my days.

He is the commander of the road,
my protector from imagined sights
sounded outside my window.

He rides shotgun beside me on the couch.
Accompanies me to town.
Slumbers beside me when I sleep.
Soothes me with his fur
beneath my roaming, roving

traveling hand.

His smallness invites care
Though he does not think it.
Deer are his equal,
Other dogs can be his nemesis.

Today he finds comfort
apart from me.
His body aches in
strange, unfamiliar places.
soft protests make their rounds.
Age is getting the better of us.

He will forgive me this moment
of dour reflection,
of lingering dread.

The Chase Game is never dull.
Curled up close,
White-whiskered,
Relevant to me,
worshipful,

I cannot let him go.

5

LOVE IS A RACE

love is a race against
the time of disadvantage.

it casts out hope
when often light is fading.

love persists.
it holds on tightly to what
was once a flittering candle.

it grows in its appreciation
of the true light of day.

love cannot be casual,
it cannot be indifferent.
it insists it must have its way
even if it is a letting go
instead of clasping to itself.

love will find a way.

love will press life beyond
even death to hold on,
to wait out faulty conclusions,
to refuse the partnership
of leaving or ending.

It runs without wavering,
Except for the pebble in its shoe.
It may slow down but will not
stand beside the road to cast it off.

Time moves and waits
for opportunity
to love more,

to love even more
deliberately.

6

LONG SHADOWS

We treat them like a dream
these vague reminiscences,
so real
sometimes,
so distant.

They nuzzle up to us,
upon a shoulder
quietly they rest,
breathing.

they wait patiently,
surprise in old haunts
we have known
together.

They are our witness post,
geodetic markers
of the spirit,

heart and
memory,
we should not disturb.

Fixed places we know,
hidden in the underbrush.

TIME'S PASSING

Wave upon wave
beats its insistence pace
upon the shore.

Blank skies
erase the horizon.
Sound and soft light
are the order of the day.

The cloud caresses the water,
and holds it softly
in its embrace.

Sometimes melodic,
its rippling tenor.

Today, strong punctuation points
at the end of each sentence.
Plots exhausted
in rock and sand.

Each a separate journey,
time's gift,
carried by unseen wind
across miles of open sea.

Only to be distributed here
at my feet, grateful for
each unexampled promise.

But another shore will one day
carry these breakers homeward.
Places I cannot see,
This water and me.

Equal parts of this inland ocean,
Moving sometimes restlessly
towards its journey's end.

8

YOU CAN'T PUSH A RIVER

Wicked ways we have
of demanding
things must happen
in our own way
instead of letting go.

Rivers flow over
undulating hills
towards an ancient
sea.

We might dam them,
but no one makes them
run back to their source
deep in the high country.

Weary, ruthless path
to contradiction,
to annoyance,
to dissatisfaction

and defeat.

The ego has twisted the
root of joy.

The farmer has written off
his crop in the likelihood of drought.

The poet stammers,
and waits.

Tantrums of the mind
from such poor beginnings.

Each object not allowed
to speak its own
language.

We translate before the word is given.

We insist compliance with
fragile branches only now
extended toward the light.

We are adrift in a world of beauty,
carried to our doorstep,

only to have it slammed shut
by our insistence

the unexpected neighbor
will never come.

While we require abundance,

we miss the tapping
on our shoulder

and the
welcoming smile.

* Title attributed to a Buddhist saying.

9

RIPPLES RUN

Ripples run
From stones cast onto
an uncertain sea.

They fly across the depths
Seeking home but unsure
if they will meet the distant shore.

They reach out never to find another.

But following in their path
they share light,
move into shadow
to become bright again.

Wave upon wave.
Recipients of brave beginnings,
Surprises set in motion
By ancient actions,

Found alive
By another's hand.

For Gordon, Jerry, Al, Arild,
Bob, Bill, and Lynn

10

LONGING

"We had such fun."
Thoughts drifting over memory.
Memories of when we were young.
When death spelled an anomaly.

It was rude then people would be lost.
Now it seems so many.
Faces laughing.
Easy enjoyment
of one another.
Innocence.

For each new generation
the gift of postponed
longevity.

We remember
in pieces,
in fragments.

Stubborn associations
with those who meant
more to us than those now.

They surrounded us.

Now we surround with our love.
We watched from outside their circle
yet always connected, always knowing
we belonged.

People of the line in the book that
cause us to remember.

People who planted knowledge
as easily as they planted flowers.

People whose trophies of life
now sit on our shelves,
waiting for our attention,
summoning back ever more
than was their intention.

These kindle flashes of time,
moments, pictures of what is past.

They remind us some cannot be forgotten
so easily. Some should not be forgotten.

Emptiness prevails.
But underneath is a knowing
that life was real and they were real.
Vanished but not gone.
At home in our hearts.

Alive still.

"We had such fun".
Gone now,
Faded,
Haunting.
Forever an unresolved chord.
The thing not quite right
with the world
that is rich and yet,
we are poorer.

We cannot have them back.
We cannot go back
to even thank those.

To steal moments
having them return
to us again.

11

FRIENDSHIP

Friendship is forged steel
joined for moments in time.

It is an unexpected surprise
at finding someone to share with.

It is that voice at the other
end of the line,
promising release.

That interested person.
Those who suffer with
And celebrate us.

It is that collegial spirit,
That ease, that casual
acknowledgment
of the other.

It remains with us

even as darkness comes.
It sees through limitation
to reward us with new eyes.
Every day, every time we meet.

Friendship initiates,
it is more than a
willingness to try.

It is to affirm
before hours are spent
finding each other
in crowds of memories.

It understands there
must be endings
without ending.
It lives beyond
occasions in life
that set people apart.

It joys in another's advantage,
finds hope when hope is draining away.
It counsels without self-interest,
and seeks out the best path
for the other to walk.

Alone, standing against the storm,
it comes often unbidden.
To share with us the nightfall.
And to welcome with us the day.

12

SQUIRRELS CAN BE HUNTED

Intently,
Bravely,
Focused.

He reconnoiters the porch,
His eyes are on the bird feeder.

Muscles tremble with strain,
Scarecrow paws pointed toward
the vacant window.

The enemy is sighted.
Great defiant whimpers arise,
guttural sounds tumble
after one another.
Pressing insistance.
Staring his jailor,
into forced entry onto
the field of battle;
the porch.

The door opens wide,
the struggle is engaged.
Reckless pursuit,
rifled escape
to the tall branches,
to the luxury of mockery
and chatter.

Decks have been cleared,
danger is abated.

Unapologetically returning
to his post, still vigilant,
proudly confident
the natural order
has not been deterred.

The canine chorus begins again
as the imagined foe
slips from the tree,
bounds on tiny feet,
repeats the contest,
the game of give-and-take.

13

THEE AND ME

This Northern coast,
how lovely.

How exquisite in its
aperture.

How powerful
and majestic
in its
overwhelming
silence and rousing
good-humored days
of prancing skyward.

Its moods are transparent,
written in the waves.

It is raw, uncertain,
playful,

seducing,
whispering,
rollicking,
beguiling.

It is the heart's last call.
It is that moment of recognition
when you know you've found
a truer home.

Patient companion,
ruler of the ancient trail,
born to me in a lifetime.

Grace-filled,
familiarity-embraced,
sensate laughter,
ease and liberty.

Watching for the
generous moment
each day brings.

Shared knowing,
Reminded memory,
Casual circumstance,
Lifted recollection.

How empty this matrix
of land and sea would be,
if not for thee.

If not for the casual

knowingness
two hearts bring,
love riding the waves
onto an antediluvian beach.

III

THE CANOE PADDLE

1

THE CANOE PADDLE

Who knows where I have traveled,
who can tell where I have been?

I've seen the lodges watching west,
I've been to continents then unknown.
Rivers, valleys, long-steeped canyons,
mother-bear home, arctic ice
and deer-home.

I've sung to soldiers in their sleep,
been beside them while they lingered,
we've hunted rice,
sought gold and treasure,
without complaint,
in silence beyond measure.

I've carried songs,
raced furlongs of rip-roar,
tabled for your trail lunches,
fought for places to end your day.

We've been a stalwart pair, haven't we?
Time to rest, time for
a day-jaunt or two,
time to reminisce.

time to stoke the fire of
a near-forgotten past,

to make eyes bright again
with the promise of adventure,
remembered.

2

CAMPFIRE COOKING

Brash,
untested,
born on the backs
of a canoe.

From the insurgency
of a backpack,
bounty comes forth.

Fish are a good denominator.
Pancakes are luscious when
spent by the luxury of a
non-travel day.

We live to venture.
We wait for elements to change.
A shift in the weather,
and we rejoice.

We wait for warmth,

watch for a cessation of the black fly,
bear mosquitos with ill humor,
carry a wasp's sting
into the next portage.

But the campfire ring
sings with the promise of food,
the delicate, delectable taste
of dehydrated squadrons
coming to our defense.

We gather to divest ourselves
of the harsh attitudes of the trail.
We celebrate sunsets on ledge rocks
with metal plates and plastic spoons,
diving eagerly into homespun food.

What keeps us from knowing
this bounty is reserved
for those who prosper
from the trail?

A salute to the cooks
who make camp worthwhile,
and who bring home a taste of the hearth
to those in far-flung, remote and empty
    places.

3

GRACIOUS BEGINNINGS

We are a band of brothers,
a fleet of sisters and mothers,
fellow-travelers into the dense
thicket of lakes and streams,
portages and places we will visit.

We live on the tide of wandered imaginings.
We wait and wrestle with uncertain weather,
our eyes always trained to an indifferent sky.

We gather our purchases,
give a pat to our canoe,
ground our packs in open ports
and fly towards the first carry.

Eager to be off,
Ready to separate
from the accustomed world
to the reckless, free-flight instigations
of nature.

There is our healer.
There is our dutiful friend.
There is the medicinal we require
from the fast flurry, from the
dour and demanding clan.

We leave our cars behind,
call to the others,
laugh with serious purpose,
watch for our compasses
to take us down the lake,
to aim us towards our first liberation.

4

BORDERLANDS

We live on two borders,
North and
near North.

It is an uneven country.
Lakes speckle the land
between.

A great sea
caresses the
rippling shore,
the ebb and flow
of ancient lava beds.

Islands populate,
sentries to the South.
They are arctic fauna,
they are soft
with flowers born
of gentler winds.

They are empty to the waves
that assault them.
They invite community.
Strangers still to the
wandering eye.

Two borders.
Remote Country
Border Crossing access
permit
required,

Then the freedom
of common ground
shared
between two
touchpoints,
foreign and
well-known.

5

LAKE OF DREAMS

Island upon island
sanctuary,
blue waters
catching a fulsome
sky.

long stretches,
wishful melodies
played on sun-swept
days.

We retreat here,
we go to get our feet wet
in rustic beauty.

Disguised bays,
Footprints of cabins,
The wash of coltish
waves,
sweeping straight

to the
Ottertrack.

Canadian mounted,
walleye-rich,
sunsets linger
in summer glory.

Exquisite beauty,
Remote,
Contained
only partially
within the imagination
of people
waiting
on
summer.

Saganaga,
Lake of Dreams.
vista-magnified,
pulse-rushing,
Lover,
Friend, and
Forecaster

of wilderness
memory
and
a shared
future.

6

FULL MOON

Brown's Island,
saturated in greens,
pines thick,
water-reflected.

A sprint to the open lake.
Palisade rising.
flat,
rock-tripe strewn.
Pull of the country.

From the top of there,
wild-er still
waters run splendiferous
along border routes.

Eagles catch more wind
and ospreys cruise past
the shell of open boats.

"It gets into you,"
this mosaic,
this time,
this pristine place.

"You can't get it out of you,"
as it romances,
seduces,
draws you in and
washes you clean.

Beguiling,
bewitching,
tender cajoling,
captivating,

It is a decoy to wonder
and rest, an allure
for the deeper
soul-parts that know
here is finding
home.

"It's no wonder
the wolf howls
at the full moon."

The siren song, the silence,
the God-grasped beauty,
star-showered
enchantment,
and love of the
unbroken trail.

Quotes by Irv Benson, taken from Duluth-News Tribune (Sunday, March 15, 1992) *"Life on the Border Bountiful for Tempest Benson,"* Saganaga Saga column by Sam Cook.

PEAR & PEACH JAM

Before the Gunflint,
lakes did not run
vertical South
to Superior.

east-west they were set.
from ridge-lines
water dove in
and flowed.

Down the Ottertrack
canoes would come,
past the long reach
of Saganaga.

10 portages to Winton,
10 back to return
to homes set back
in the woods,
nestled to

sandy beaches,
projected onto
shelf-rock.

Wilderness families,
tutored children,
tested and strong women,
determined men.

Some eccentric,
some homespun,
grabbing for what they
could from a land where
wild geese would fly.

Moose pups,
wolf children,
beaver and otter playmates,
bear cubs licking the honey
syrup from off their hands.

Curious companions to
youngsters separated
from their kindred kind.

Opened cups of pear and peach
from a generous spirit,
giving from their sacrifice,
their meager bounty.

joyful present,
exuberance,
extravagance

from simple means.

In honor of Irv and Tempest Benson and all
the others who settled here, came out in
the spring from its winters, raised family
and shared hospitality.

8

GREAT-LAKES RENDEZVOUS

Stomping ground of the fur trade.
Meeting place.
Grand archway of
water and sky,

Drawn from ancient distances.
Met in shallow waters,
Eyes always
on the far-reaching shore,
deserved,
able,
hardened,
stout subjects of paddle
and pull.

Penitent traders
thrown from
Superior's severe
waters
up onto a

friendly beach,
roustabout
comaraderie.

Compressed joy.

Moments met.
Delirious homecoming.
Destined for autumn
to retreat
back
home.

Erst the winter winds teach them.
Distracted for too long
They advance into snow.

9

FOG LANDS

It reaches its watery paw
out onto the road,
before it escapes to the hills,
and douses the land
with dimness
and obscurity.

It envelops.
It shuts down sight,
attunes the ear,
particularizes the senses
to what is felt and
intuited.

Pockets can break
into sunshine,
while around,
thick walls of
cloud and gloom.

Anxious loved ones
search the fog lands
for return of family
from the burly,
refusing
void.

Old-timers remember.

Alone, on a rolling sea,
the deaf quiet,
the unsettled heart,
the possessed calm.

The tightened grip on the
tiller's disinterested
handle.

Ears keenly alert for the music
of passing islands,
the echo-alert to breaks
in the shoreline,
to the bays turning inward.

Sharp eyes seeking
fingers of rock,
protection from release
into the boundless blue
that takes no prisoner,
adrift in immensity.

To keep one's wits,
to stop the one-lunger
occasionally,

to wait out
the silence,
to mark one's place,
to dampen rashness,
is a sailor's prerogative.

To wait for the sun to arrive.
To believe one can be at home
in a mystified world
where shore is but
a determination,

where the hearth remains
a stubborn memory
that will not let go.

Alone and unassisted,
without demarcation or line,
caught in uncertainty,
in the ambiguity of daylight.

purpose is driven
slowly and attentively,
cautiously and adroitly

and yet,

it runs to
an unseemly
tide.

WHICHWOOD

Witch wood crackles,
taunted by paper birch,
underneath,
in its shadows.

It offers itself to the flame.

It leaves the obscurity
of trees covered in pine-pitch,
the dark spruce,
midnight divination.

Wasted wood,
transformed into treasure.
Thousands of its tiny branches
finding a home
in the fire.

It births the comforts of the trail.
It offers to the weary traveler

the promise of moonlight,
the beaver slap out on the bay
as the shadowed canyons of night
slip in to overwhelm the day.

Which Wood is chosen,
delegated,
valued,
taken by eager hands,
forged into bundles,
cast against the rain storm,
dryness personified.

So quickly it ends.
So soon it is forgotten
In the firelight's first glow.

Blanketed by chunks of wood
more willing to sustain
the magic of stars
and the loon's soft call.

11

RENEGADE

Sallow now,
burnished by the warp of life,
retreated,
found in low places.

once emblazoned,
crazy vision,
steeled for life on the trail.

a companion to the open road.
watchful willingness,
rushing in,
captured intention
waiting for the starter's pistol.

Eyes that still light,
a mind that still flares,
with un-abandoned excess.

ferreting out hot peppers

and jalapeno from allspice
and cumin.

Brave and bold refusal,
Wanderlust has never left them.
They prevail even still
within the bordered resolve
of tested spirits.

12

FALL WEATHER

Laughing uproariously,
it is a trickster.

It seduces us with days of warmth,
promises us more sunshine,
offers us discordant paths
through forests of maple
and cathedrals of pine.

It wraps itself around us and tarries,
not to do harm but to bless us.
To take to the woods,
to scent the crispness
of autumn is a delight.

Paths unworn from recent travel.
Lakes are untrammeled.
Campsites are organized affairs
without the competition of
erstwhile migrant travelers.

Nights are slept in soundly.
There is magic to the waters.
The sun-drenched trees
caress every shore.

Color abounds in the hills,
populates the ancient trails,
rises up to the ridge lines,
blends with the water
near shore.

We wait for the first frost.
It chases many away.
We wonder when
winter will descend.

It is stolen property we trespass on.

We have it all for our keeping,
for one day or for a length of time,
until beaver move deftly into their houses,
until bluebills fly South with certainty.

Until the land turns over
into winter white.

IV

THE HAUNTING MOON

1

THE HAUNTING MOON

Fear are wolves in the shadows,
moving amongst the trees.

Fear is the catch in your breath,
the unspoken word that must not
be uttered.

Fear breathes into us and stops our
every movement.

Fear constricts and from imagined chasms
paints pictures, that startle and dismay.

Fear is not contained.
It penetrates into the gloom to
race on the wind of our desires
and failure to meet them.

Fear is a friend that occasionally will
come for our benefit.

Fear lives in the beams cast by
discomforted darkness.
Real enough not to be real.
Real enough not to be dismissed.

On nights such as this
Walk carefully.
Know that in the light of day,
fear can be silenced.

It walks but not so loudly.
It breathes but not so incessantly.
It cripples but does not kill.
It whispers but will not shout.

Fear is the afterthought of imagination.
The hobgoblin of minds that will choose
not to rest.

Howling, they greet the predators
and welcome them, even into the
heart of a camp, where the fire
spurns off heat and light.

2

SHORE LIGHT

Lakers make their way
bashed by unrefined wave,
a carnival of lights
set on an uneven
horizon.

Deliberate speed,
cruising majesty,
intentional,
cautious,
committed.

She runs to the Bay,
glutting her hold
with commerce,
fades South
and has the world
to her advantage.

I light a tree

in the hopes
someone there
will watch
as it rolls by.

A bit of home,
a beacon,

the shout of Christmas
brightness,
an unspoken
bond between
us.

A touch of humanity
on an inland sea.

3

CRAZY FEAR

It is the gentle persuasion of dread.
The smarmy feeling in the pit of one's gut
that things will go awry.

It can scream at us, fighting for its own
    survival.
It is the lead wolf snarling and licking its
    chops.
It travels far and near.
It cannot rest.

It watches and waits.
It is tone deaf to reason.
It flies in the face of all logic.

To find a home in our sinew and senses.
It traces its bony fingers through the hair
of our memories
and our futures.

It is our mate on ventures into the unknown.
It lies to us, caresses us, tells us we are weak.
It reminds us that someone else
must complete the journey.

It resides on the hardscrabble
shores of our life.

It licks like fire at the soft wooden resin
of our ambitions, hopes, and dreams.
It is a canker on the roof
of our mouths, teasing us
with an oily pain.

It finds a home in our hesitancies.
It must be stopped.
Emboldened, it will feed
on its own blood and substance.

It will cripple as it attempts,
in its wayward way, to mend.

It is both ghastly and ghostly.
We can see it intends
to surround us
and to insulate.

It is a gifted Lippizaner cantering
in rhyme with the music.
Its mighty flanks will crush us
against the boards of our desires.

We must float lightly.

We must gather in its message,
bend to its hopes,
Watch over the mystery.
Embrace the deeper melodies
of our hearts.

We must not falter.
We must enjoin and tell ourselves
and the world
we will not drift
into obscurity.

That wolf snarling must be subdued,
not with a club
but with firm assurance.
We are yet still masters.

We must stand over it,
hear its guttural warnings,
feel the cool ruff of its neck
as fur clasps in our hands.

We must stare it in the eye
and say, "Not today."

Tomorrow may be another opportunity,
Another opening when our backs are turned.
But right now, in this encounter,
we must be the alpha,
the lead dog, the one
in front on the traces!

Sniffing out home,
finding direction,

knowing where
danger lurks.

The rest of our pack-dogs will follow.

Beneath the soft light of the moon,
the harshness of the cold,
the bitterness of the day,
we are the ones that must
bring order to a vast land.

A wilderness of our own making.

4

CHILD LEAVING

They've left so many times before,
this child of mine.

Off to take each impatient step,
uncertain at first, gathering steam.

Always away, towards
eager participation in life's
array of challenges and delectables.

Coming home,
A backward turn,

Moments of definition
when I know
I am not their rock
but their resting place.

Grace-notes they offer,
tributes to memory,

the time I have invested.

Gracious glances
before moving on.

Privileged knowing,
never forgotten,
a trust I have paid into
for all these years.

5

HARDSCRABBLE

Hardscrabble rock
Inert, incapable of grasping
Anything but the warmth of the sun.

While overhead a cougar moves,
Watchful, waiting, ever mindful
of the changing kaleidoscope
of color and movement.

It walks with purpose, yet aimlessly.
A flick of its tail indicates interest.
Its fierce teeth gnarl at danger.

It is a fugitive presence
As it crosses the yard,
moving always on.

But its footpads guard but a small space.
As it crouches, sometimes lays down,
Sometimes embraces the ground,

And sometimes looks skyward.

Wild, still free. Roaming
in our imagination.

Resident of this northern shore.

6

4SIGHT

It haunts me still
that rich opportunity,
that chance worth taking.

Withdrawn, I let slip
life's invitation.
I withdrew from the field.
My vision did not carry me
across the finish.

Practical thoughts intruded.
Resources were dimmed low.

I have only the ghosts of
misspent fortune to
walk beside me.

Oh, to wake to the possibility
when it is so close to the touch.

To see in life's invitation
what is for the greater good.

To witness to pure gold,
when I see only the gold of
fools and reckless spending.

To wait out the night,
to embrace the darkness,
to let the future tease me
and to let myself be caught.

How principled,
how right-minded,
up-standing and
true-blue.

Land I shall never wander,
hopes now ever more diminished.
Seedlings never grown
to towering pine,

because they were never
planted.

7

GREATNESS

A songbird perches
bravely
outside my
winter window.

It sings to my woods,
chirps to my morning.

It has decided
to befriend me.

It looks inward
to the glass.

Is it me he sees or but
his own reflection?

Greatness is his familiarity,
his willingness to come so close.

Without seeing me in
the blank reflections
of my window?

Whether I see him or not.

It doesn't matter.
Such a rare sight,
so normal
in the course
of a day's pleasure.

So rare a find in the
mystery of why he has chosen me.

Routinely, he makes his rounds now.
I can almost come to expect it.

8

MY GUITAR STILL WAITS

Filled with unrepentant promises
I postponed my days of
entering into life.

I grasped at moments,
Eager to deflect from
my children's wishes
to go another round,
outrageous play,
unbridled fun.

Joy was there
in their offering.

Mine was a retreat
into the quiet room
of dreams and
indulgent practice.

Moments escaped and lost

appear to me now
as time-less energy.

I wanted relief.
But now I see
so clearly, childhoods
come and gone,

opportunity vanished,
promises delayed
and put-on-hold.

Martin expects an answer
Now that moments trip into days.
How elusive its been,
this strand between
sea and shore.

My roving eye turns to other children
who wait for me to come out and play.
My melody never lost to the silences.

So uncertain the days,
So rich with promise,
A second chance
at celebrity,

Called up to the Major League
when I thought only the minor
would do.

9

I WILL COME TO COMFORT YOU

I am alone,
Lost between
the staccato points
of my life.

I have reason to celebrate
but hold my glass by myself.

I am sad but cannot fill it.
Lost but no one searches for me.
I am waiting for rescue but look
to an empty sky.

I am anxious, eager, hopeful,
agitated, at odds with myself.

Disappointed by love.
Haunted by dreams
unfulfilled,
broken steps,

I have taken.

You come to comfort me.
You bring me the exotic
tastes that enflame me,
cause me to feel passion,
accompany me, befriend
and caress my disquietude.

You remind me of home.
Faces from the past are never
so far away. They linger on the
gentle aromatic streams of memory.

You join me in my celebrations,
journey with me in the silent
and sometimes corruptible
dark spaces.

You remove the cares of the day
in quiet conversation and in
rollicking good company.

There has never been but one glass.
We meet as two.

There to celebrate
or to console each other,
touched by what perhaps
is only a slightly
overindulgent hand.

10

CROFTVILLE ROAD

A gentle persuasion of road
cut into the rocks,
long-lining the shore.

Old fish houses
neatly crumbling,
sea-worthy boats
displayed
from
bygone day.

Old-fashioned,
Old-time,
Old-fangled,
forget-me-nots
flowers growing
amidst the stone.

Creeks tired from the
rush of spring,

insinuate
themselves
down to the
shore,

cradled by latticework
of neat boulders,
ledges of shale and
cobblestone,
time-worn.

Quiet waters among the cliff
faces touch the edges
of a shoulder-less byway.

Traces of the past,
intimate reminder,
highway shielded,
struggling to fit
itself

to an unsteady
present.

11

DELAYED SUMMER

Dark skies persist,
Ink-stained,
alligator clouds
low and thick.

Grim reminders of
cold temperatures.
I watch my thermometer
religiously.

Iris' are coming slowly.
Marigolds hold on.
Leaves of birch,
reluctantly coming
to full throttle.

Lovers stroll beside
a serious harbor
with sweater and
sweatshirt on.

Incongruous dress,
for reverie.

Watching each day,
for a break in the
weather,

Tasted only,
appetizers without
the full meal.

Leaving us unsatisfied
in waiting,
in searching for why
the waiter seems to be
ignoring us.

NIGHT MYSTERY

Up the canyons of the Quetico
The night is still, the moon is high:
Racing with the silence
A loon call pressed against the ridges
Far away yet close it flies.

It speaks to wild places,
It beckons to the Great Unknown
Country I will never travel,
Alone still not alone.

Rising up in throaty distance,
Wildness here and on display.
Flute softness among the rocks,
Ancient sound of ancient days.

Waiting for my heart's echo,
Returning to its purest melodies.
Finding pleasure in this moment,
Finding joy in mystery.

ACKNOWLEDGMENTS

To my friends in Grand Marais and elsewhere who encouraged me and who provided guidance along the way.

To my family who bless me in my writing.

To those who have been kind enough to assist in the editing of this book. Thank you.

To Robert Service, an early inspiration. His poetry is magic.

To Vellum for making publishing projects so much more manageable.

To pro_ebookcovers for designing the cover for this book.

To BrainyQuotes for the opening passage by Houdini.

To readers who invest themselves as they make many of these images and ideas their own. Cheers!

IF YOU ENJOYED THIS BOOK, please write a brief review on Amazon. Just type in *Who's Watching Whoo?* You can also check any number of stars and remain anonymous if you wish.

It is the lifeblood of every author to gain such reviews.

INTERESTED IN immediate updates to everything I've written? New blogs? Fresh insight? Ideas applied to life? Go to my website: johnbragstad.com to sign-up and subscribe.

No obligation. Easy to subscribe and
unsubscribe. And welcome aboard!

ABOUT COMPASS SEASON:
COMPANION TO WHO'S WATCHING WHOO?

"Bragstad was a Boundary Waters and Quetico canoe guide and had over 25 years as a licensed marriage and family counselor. His experiences provide depth, insight, motivation, beauty, and comfort to readers." *Northern Wild*

"Aldo Leopold (Sand County Almanac) may be the master of nature writing, and Gary Chapman (The 5 Love Languages) may be the master of "relationship writing." But no one weaves the two realms together as neatly and poignantly as John Bragstad in **Compass Season**." *Amazon Review*

"I believe its greatest value is as a book that you can pick up when you have only 10 minutes but know you need slowing down and re-centering." Amazon Reviews

"Since receiving this book in the mail one week ago, I have found it very hard to put down; it draws me back. It is to experience beauty." *Amazon Review*

"**Compass Season** is a beautiful read for those who love to be pleasantly surprised with the peace and meaning found along life's path, one that you'll reread often." *Amazon Review.*

"What a surprise of a book! Not at all what I expected, but once you start reading, you are hooked!" *Amazon Review*

> "This book is a gem. It's like the reward from a long hike to an alpine lake sitting on your coffee table." *Amazon Review*

"While calming to read, this book provides perspective for life's challenges while reconnecting us with nature and our internal resources. I highly recommend this book!" *Amazon Review*

"A hot cup of coffee and this book is the perfect start to the day! Inspiring imagery and beautifully written to provide applicable reflections to everyday life!" *Amazon Review*

John Bragstad enjoyed three seasons as a canoe guide in the Minnesota Arrowhead country and on the Churchill River system in Saskatchewan, Canada.

He was a therapist and guide to many as a licensed Marriage and Family counselor in Minnesota for over 25 years.

He is trained in cognitive-behavioral therapy (CBT) and organizational development in addition to being a certified life coach.

Before this, he was a teacher /school counselor, and parish pastor.

He lives in Grand Marais, Minnesota - gateway to the Boundary Waters Canoe Area Wilderness (BWCAW) of North America.

NATURE POETRY ON THE WING

READINGS TO RELAX BY

Who's Watching Whoo? It's about many of life's simple things. It asks us to be humble, to walk quietly. If we pay attention, there are answers at the end of a sometimes long, broken trail. There are signs in the underbrush, broken twigs, and brush-strokes of the tip of wings on fallen snow.

Free verse poetry, in my experience, has been a rewarding way of getting to the basics in a short space of time. They paint a picture, offer some glimmer of insight, and are gone, and we move on, but never quite.

I envision readers looking at **Who's Watching Whoo** when they want to break away from the crazy rush of their everyday lives. We dream of getting out into nature, chasing the city away even for a short time. Perhaps this book will be one way of opening the window, even if it is just a crack.

Nights have been a challenge for me. I've learned not to fight with sleep but to enjoy the quiet, meditative moments. If this is your experience, perhaps this book might be a worthy companion.

And for anyone who lives within the Canoe Country's memory, perhaps this book will fan the flames once again. Many of these verses center around Saganaga, Lake Superior, and places north of the Grand Portage. May you find the quiet here as it once found you in wild places.

23396333R00094